Amaz

Fire Max 11

User Guide

**The Complete Instruction Manual For Amazon
Fire Max 11 Tablet For Beginners And Seniors
With Useful Updates, Tips And Tricks**

Peter Ashes

Table of Contents

CHAPTER 1

Introducing Amazon Fire Max 11

Amazon's Fire Max 11, which includes a keyboard and stylus and costs less than an iPad, is the best tablet value ever. Twelve years after Jeff Bezos introduced the first Fire Tablet, Amazon is producing a plastic-free version of its budget-friendly tablets. The aluminum Fire Max 11 is here to introduce itself. The Fire Max 11 lives up to its name as Amazon's largest tablet to date, including an 11-inch screen. Amazon's Kevin Keith, Amazon devices vice president, explains over Zoom that the company is responding to consumer demand for larger tablet screens.

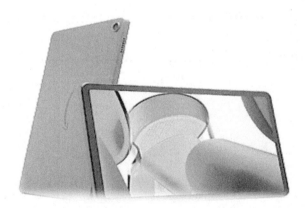

like an iPad or the OnePlus Pad. For an additional $329.98, Amazon offers a package deal that includes a stylus in addition to a keyboard/trackpad accessory. Both are significantly cheaper than the base model, 10.9-inch iPad from Apple's latest generation, which begins at $449.

Specifications

- Display: 11 inches (2,048 by 1,920 pixels)
- Chip: MediaTek MT8188J 2.2GHz
- Storage and RAM: 4GB RAM, 64 or 128GB (up to 1TB with microSD).
- Battery life: 14 hours
- 8-megapixel cameras in the back
- 8-megapixel front-facing camera
- Fingerprint reader

There's an 8-megapixel camera on the front and back for selfies and video chats. A pair of Dolby Atmos speakers are mounted on the side. The inclusion of a fingerprint reader in the power button is another first for a Fire Tablet. Storage expansion (by microSD card, up to 1TB) is hands-down my favorite feature. The operating system for the Fire Max 11 is FireOS 8, a variant of Android 11. Anyone who has used a Fire Tablet before knows what to anticipate: Despite being a marketplace for Amazon's media offerings

2

(Kindle books, Prime videos, Prime Music, etc.), the Appstore is still understocked in comparison to rivals like Google Play and the Apple App Store.

However, the Fire Max 11 has a Show Mode that, when used, transforms the tablet into a smart display similar to the Echo Show and enables hands-free Alexa operation. The Fire Max 11 can be distinguished from the Fire HD 10 Plus by its compatibility with external accessories like a keyboard and a pen. The keyboard is a two-piece device that snaps onto the Fire Max 11 with the help of some pogo pins and magnets on the back. One half of the keyboard features a standard QWERTY keyboard and trackpad, while the other serves as an adjustable kickstand. A comparison to Apple's Magic Keyboard Folio for the tenth-generation iPad seems inevitable. The trackpad is gesture-enabled, and the keyboard features 15 pre-programmed shortcut keys (located above the number row).

Starting at just $329.99, the Amazon Fire Max 11 tablet, keyboard, and pen combination is an incredible value. Over Zoom, Keith demonstrated the multitasking capabilities of the Fire Max 11 and how the "Fire Max 11's MFA stylus pen" could be utilized for on-screen handwriting detection in text fields.

Performance

There is a catch with that pricing...The Fire Max 11's modest price tag doesn't translate to a sluggish performance. Keith assures me that the Fire Max 11's 2.2GHz MediaTek chipset makes it "50 percent faster" than the Fire HD 10 Plus.

The Fire Tablet's 7.5mm aluminum body is the thinnest of any Fire tablet to date, and the device as a whole weighs in at a feathery 420 grams. The "alumino-silicate glass" on the Fire Max 11 is "3x as durable as the iPad 10.9" (10th generation)," as claimed by Amazon. That sounds great. The 11-inch screen's resolution of 2,000 by 1,200 won't compare to the high-end iPads' OLED or mini-LED, but it should still be quite sharp. Wi-Fi 6 is supported, and the battery can last for up to 14 hours on a single charge.

The aluminum-bodied Amazon Fire Max 11 tablet can be had for as little as $229.99.

CHAPTER 2

Install Google Play Store

Tips for getting started

1. If you aren't using adoptable storage (where your SD card storage is combined with your internal storage, for instance), remove the microSD card from your Fire tablet. The Play Store and its prerequisite apps can be installed automatically on the external SD incase you don't remove it. Once the software has been installed, the microSD card should be returned to its original slot.

2. Even after Play Store installation will allow you to manage a Fire tablet using Google Family Link. Create a child profile on your Max 11 instead.

3. It's possible that apps downloaded from the Play Store won't function with the Amazon Kids+ subscription.

4. Due to the fact that Fire tablets are not Google Play SafetyNet approved, some apps are unavailable on Fire tablets. A prime illustration would be Netflix. You can find these programs in the Amazon Appstore or on APKMirror.

Permit Installation from Unknow sources

To access the Security & Privacy menu, enter Settings from the primary Home screen. On older models, "Security" might have been omitted.

- Select the option that reads "Apps from Unknown Sources."

PRIVACY

Location-Based Services
Share your approximate location using Wi-Fi with third-party apps and websites.

Apps from Unknown Sources
Allow installation of applications that are not from Appstore.

App pinning
Off

App pinning Preferences

Credential Storage
View and store digital certificates that are typically used for VPN and enterprise Wi-Fi access.

Device Administrators
See which applications are authorized as device administrators for your Fire.

- Turn on Silk's "Apps from Unknown Sources" option.

 Install unknown apps

Silk Browser

108.2.18.5359.220.10

Allow from this source

Your tablet and personal data are more vulnerable to attack by unknown apps. By installing apps from this source, you agree that you are responsible for any damage to your tablet or loss of data that may result from their use.

Apps from Unknown Sources can be enabled with a single switch rather than individual app selections on older devices running incompatible OS. As a result, the third step is no longer necessary.

You can now access the APKs required to launch the Google Play Store and begin downloading them.

Download the APK Files!

- Four APK files will need to be downloaded through the Fire tablet's built-in Silk browser. Copying the URLs here or, much better, visiting this page in the Silk browser and clicking the links will allow you to quickly and conveniently download the files. This is the quickest route to the download pages.
1. Google Account Manager (APK).
2. Google Services Framework APK.
3. Google Play Services APK.
4. Google Play Store APK
- Then, when the download page opens on Silk, you can go to the bottom and click Download APK. A warning window will appear once you've begun the download, explaining that the file could potentially cause damage to your computer. Don't worry about it; just click OK.
- After the download is complete, redo the process for the remaining APK files.

Install APK files for the Google Play Store

- After everything has finished downloading, open Docs on your Fire tablet.

- Press local storage.
- Click the Downloads folder.

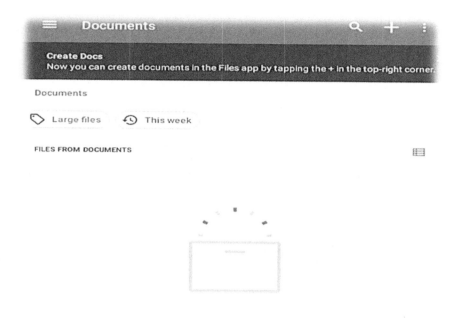

Here you'll find the APKs you downloaded earlier. Tap on each one to set them up. Make careful you get the APKs in the order they appear below.

Installation should be in the following order:

1. First download the APK file for Google Account Manager (com.google.android.gsf.login).

2. The next application package (APK) is Google Services Framework (com.google.android.gsf).

11

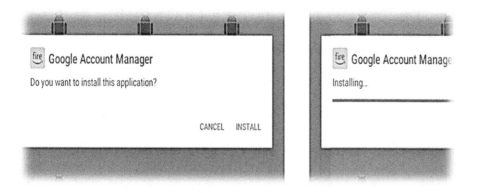

3. After that, the APK file for Google Play Services (com.google.android.gms)

4. Last but not least, the com.android.vending APK for the Google Play Store.

Your tablet and personal data are more vulnerable to attack by unknown apps. By installing this app, you agree that you are responsible for any damage to your tablet or loss of data that may result from its use.

CANCEL   CONTINUE

Get the Files Setup

- Tap Install on the next screen. The name of the APK you're installing will appear in the top left corner. Make sure you're installing in the recommended order.

If the Install button is grayed out and you can't click it, try turning your screen off and back on. Once you've done that, you can unlock your Fire tablet, at which point the Install button will turn orange.

Following the aforementioned procedures, the Google Play Store will become available in the app drawer.

- Launch it on your computer, and then sign in using your Google credentials.
- The program can initially not function as expected but bear with it until it does.
- Automatic updates will be applied to the Google Play Store and Google Play Services.
- Once the Google Play Store is set up, various apps can be downloaded and installed from the store onto your Max 11.

Set up parental controls

- To access the settings, swipe down from the screen's top.
- Select the "Parental" tab.
- Turn on Parental Controls by toggling the switch.
- Put in a password and then double-check it.
- Tap the end.
- A lock icon will appear in the upper right corner of the display once parental controls are activated.

Simple parental settings for Amazon Fire tablets let you limit access to:

1. Amazon Online Store
2. Web browsing
3. Email, Address Book, and Scheduler
4. Sharing social networks
5. The camera
6. Books, apps, and other sorts of information.

The following can be secured behind a parental control password:

1. Buying stuff from the Amazon app store or other Amazon digital stores on your device.

2. Streaming Prime Video movies and shows.

3. Joining Wi-Fi.

4. Authorizing Location Services.

How to limit your child's tablet use and establish a bedtime routine:

- To activate the Set a Curfew function, simply tap the corresponding switch.
- Hit Curfew schedule.
- You get to decide which days and hours your kid can't use the gadget.
- If you want to unlock a device after curfew, the password set under parental controls must be entered.

Controls child tablet

1. In order to keep tabs on your kid's Amazon Fire usage, you can toggle the switch next to Monitor This Profile.

2. A parent and kid emblem will appear at the very top of a profile that is being monitored.

- Visit the Activity Center section of Your Devices within Manage Your Content and Devices to view the data.
- Access detailed information on your child's app usage, reading progress, and content consumption.

Amazon FreeTime

- To access the settings, swipe down from the screen's top.
- Press Profiles & Family Library.
- Choose a child profile.
- Select Subcribe Amazon FreeTime Unlimited.
- Choose a subscription plan:
1. Child plan ($4.99/mo; $2.99/mo for Prime members): If you want to give one child in your family access to Kindle FreeTime Unlimited but not another, or if you only have one child registered for Amazon FreeTime, you can do so.
2. The Family Plan Costing $119 annually or $83 annually for Prime members, is available for purchase for $9.99 per month. Up to four children in your home can be covered by a single subscription.

How to Use Amazon FreeTime

- Choose the FreeTime app.

- Choose a child profile.

- Press Set Daily Goals & Time Limits and use the sliders to determine the maximum amount of time they can spend each day using the device and its various applications.

- Hit Turn off by time to stop them from using the tablet in the wee hours of the morning.

- Select Smart Filters from the menu under Manage your Child's Content to establish an age limit for the types of content your child can view.

Set up Adult profile

Creating an adult profile on an Amazon Fire tablet is more involved than creating a child's profile. This is because Amazon requires at least one adult member per household to be enrolled. However, this process is swift. And it's all right there on the same menu for your convenience.

- To access the notification drawer, swipe down from the top of the screen.

- To access more options, swipe down from the screen's top once more.

- In the lower right edge of your display, you'll find a little human icon. Click it.
- Pick Create Account.
- Hit OK.
- Pick Create an additional adult profile.
- A password prompt will appear.
- If you're prompted, have the second adult take the tablet.
- We're going to require the other adult to log into his Amazon account.
- Take the displayed instructions to finish.

The invitee has 14 days to respond. Once someone has joined your Amazon Household, you will be able to view their profile on your tablet. Remember that the maximum number of adults allowed in an Amazon Household is 2.

Set up a child profile

A child's profile is significantly simpler to set up. Let me explain.

- To access the notification drawer, swipe down from the upper part of the screen.

- To access further options, simply swipe down from the screen's top once more.
- In the lower right edge of your screen, you'll find a little human icon. Click it.
- Pick Create Account.
- Hit OK.
- Pick Add Child Profile.
- Please provide your first name and date of birth. Pick a picture to represent yourself.
- Hit the Add Profile option.

Switch profiles

Changing between profiles is simple when you've set them up.

- To access the notification drawer, swipe down from the top of the screen.
- If you want more choices, swipe down from the top of the display again.
- In the lower right edge of your display, you'll find a little human icon. Click it.

- Choose the user profile you wish to use by tapping on it.

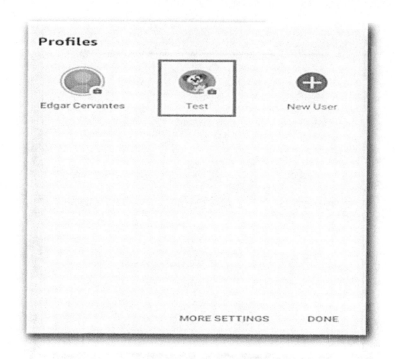

Delete profile

- Launch the Amazon App Store. Use the tab with three lines for options.

- To delete an account, head to Account > Manage your Household and click Remove next to the relevant user name.

Remove Child Profile

- Click the "Settings" button.
- Choose the Profiles and Family Library.
- Press the preferred profile to remove.
- Go to manage child profile.

21

- Pick remove child profile.
- Press remove.

Connect to charger

Tablets are easily damaged by sudden shifts in temperature, so make sure they are kept in a comfortable range.

- Separate your gadget from its charging wire and power supply. Take the tablet away from the wireless charging dock or mat.
- Hold the power button down until the device restarts, or for a total of 40 seconds.
- Put the charging cable back into its proper place, plug the power adapter into an electrical outlet, and reconnect your smartphone.

While your Fire tablet is being charged, the indication light will be orange. You can be able to get a new tablet under warranty if your current one still won't charge.

CHAPTER 3

Update Software

- Connect to Wi-Fi. To download and install software updates, an internet connection is required.

- Tune the controls by Swiping down from the upper part of the home screen will bring up the notification drawer.

- Select "Settings" by tapping the cogwheel icon.

- In the "Settings" menu, press "Device Options" (or "Device" on older models) and scroll down to it.

- Selecting "System Updates," or "Software Updates,". To see if there are any newer versions, tap on it.

- You will be requested to download and install the update.

- The update could take a while to finish, so be sure your tablet is either plugged in or has a full battery.

- Activating the update process will cause your tablet to download the updated files and install them automatically. There will be a restart of the tablet required for the update to take effect, so please be patient.

- Verify that "Your device is up to date" or a similar message appears when you navigate to "Settings" > "Device Options" > "System Updates" to see if the update was successful.

Change Book theme

Changing the font or size of the text is one way to make reading more enjoyable. Themes allow you to customize many aspects of your document, such as the line spacing in a book.

- To make a modification, go to settings.
- Use the Aa key to switch to the Themes panel. There will be a range of sizes to choose from, from compact standard and large.
- For instance, pressing "large" will result in wider gaps between the lines, while selecting "compact" will narrow them.
- Pick the topic that best addresses your requirements. To switch themes, simply repeat the previous procedures.

Change font Size

You can make the text bigger and bolder if you find it difficult to read the smaller font size.

- Tap the upper part of the screen when you open a book.
- To adjust the Kindle's font size, press the Aa button, choose Font, and then use the sliders provided.
- The Bold settings can also be fiddled with (but not in a side-loaded MOBI book).
- To modify the size, tap the corresponding plus or minus sign.
- Remember that the Kindle's screen can be resized for easier reading.

Customize Language

- First close all open Apps.
- Access the notification tray by swiping down from the top of the screen.
- You can access the settings menu via a shortcut at the upper part of this panel.
- There are submenus for "Device," "Personal," and "System".

- To change your device's keyboard and language, go to the "Personal Settings" section and scroll down.

- Here we have the choice of switching the language settings so that content can be displayed in several tongues.

- Choose your language from the menu bar at the top of the screen.

- Clicking this again will take you to the language selection screen you saw when you first set up your device.

Reset Kindle

- Turn it on by pressing and holding the "Power" button for a few seconds.

- Second, bring up the device menu by swiping down from the top of the screen; then, press "More" to bring up the settings.

- Go to the "Device" menu, then "Reset to Factory Defaults."

- After pressing "Erase Everything," press "Yes" to confirm. The Kindle powers down and returns to its original configuration.

- Hold on for roughly 5 min. After the tablet reboots, it will ask you to press a network to join.

- Enter the password for your wireless network after pressing it. The tablet will ask you to register your Kindle once it has established a network connection.

- Type in your Amazon account's email and password, and then click "Register." After setting up an account, the Kindle will guide you through the configuration process. All content downloaded from the Kindle Store or stored in the cloud will still be accessible, notwithstanding the loss of any local files.

Soft reset

- First, press and hold the "Power" button for twenty seconds.

- Let go of the "Power" button until the charging indicator light turns on.

- If you want to restart your tablet, simply press the "Power" button a third time.

Change Wallpaper

- Launch the Settings menu.

- Then, go to Settings and press Home Screen & Wallpaper.

- Navigate to Home Screen Settings.
- Look for the More Wallpapers option and tap it.
- Then, select your preferred wallpaper by scrolling the available options to the right or left.
- Then, after a little pause, press the Apply button.
- As you can see, the wallpaper that was previously loading on your Home Screen has been replaced with one randomly selected from the available options.

However, the second method provided below is for those who like to personalize their Home Screen Wallpaper by selecting an image from the Gallery.

- Enter the Gallery option in the Home Screen Settings menu.
- Press Gallery again to enter the section containing the required image.
- Choose a photo by clicking on it once.
- Then, hit the Blur symbol and move the selector to the right or left to blur the current Home Screen wallpaper.
- Click the Apply button to permanently store your modifications.

- Hit the Home Screen menu and hold off for a second.

Wonderful! You can confidently change the Home Screen background now that you know how.

Lock Sim Card

- Enter the Settings menu.
- Go to Settings, then choose Privacy and Security.
- After that, click More Settings to access the configuration menu.
- Select the Credentials and Encryption option now.
- Now is the time to press Set SIM Lock 1 from the menu.
- The SIM card lock must then be activated through the adjacent switch.
- Enter your personal SIM card PIN in the final field. SIM Lock Code for Amazon Fire Max 11.

Show Mode

In 2018, Amazon announced Show Mode as a free software upgrade for Fire tablets, allowing them to mimic the functionality of the Echo Show. Without purchasing an Echo Show, you can still use Alexa to ask questions, play media, and manage compatible smart home devices with your voice. Show Mode was introduced alongside a dedicated Show Mode Charging Dock for the Amazon Fire tablet; however, the dock is not required to use Show Mode. Show Mode can be used in three different ways on a Fire tablet.

First, consult Alexa.

- Tell Alexa to activate Show Mode on your Fire tablet. The user interface will then transition into Show Mode.
- Say "Alexa, exit Show Mode" to end Show Mode.

Second, you can use the shortcut in the settings menu.

- To access the fast settings menu on your Fire tablet, slide down twice from the top of the screen.
- There's an option to toggle Show Mode on and off in the list of configurations. If you click it, Show Mode will activate.
- Use the same double-swipe motion and press the Show Mode toggle one more to turn off Show Mode.

CHAPTER 4

Set Warm Light

- Go to settings by swiping down from the top of the display.

- Under "Warmth," move the slider to a temperature that suits you. The image below doesn't show it, but when the screen temperature rises, the color of the light will get more orange.

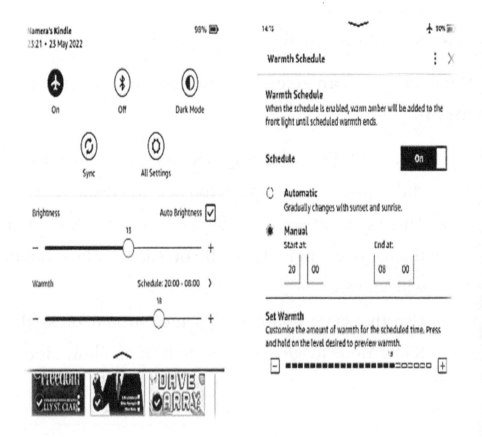

- When you open the Warmth Schedule page by tapping Schedule, you can choose Automatic or enter specific times for when you'd like the warm light to turn on.

- The latter provides warm light after sunset.

When Wi-Fi is enabled, the sunset time is determined using the current time. Your Kindle will utilize default times (such as 7 a.m. and 7 p.m.) if you turn this feature off.

Adjust Auto Brightness

The screen brightness adjusts automatically utilizing an ambient light sensor with auto-brightness. However, if you're unhappy with the current level of brightness, you can increase it manually, just like with older Kindles.

- To access the settings menu, swipe down from the top of your screen. The Brightness segment is located above the warmth slider.

- Slide the slider with your fingers to the desired setting. You can even go all the way down to zero if you want.

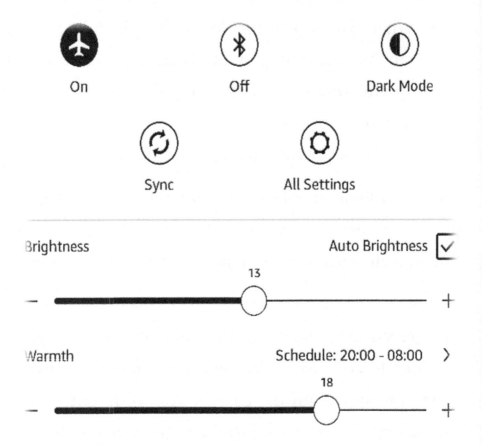

- It should be noted that this does not disable auto-brightness. To achieve this, check the option next to Auto Brightness.

Turn on Dark Mode

You might choose to turn on your dark mode instead of reading at night with warm light. This flips the colors on your website so that the backdrop is black and the lettering is white. The screen is still lit from the front. You wouldn't be able to see it anyway, but the darkness means the light is much more muffled. If you're lying next to someone in bed, dark mode is less likely to wake them up.

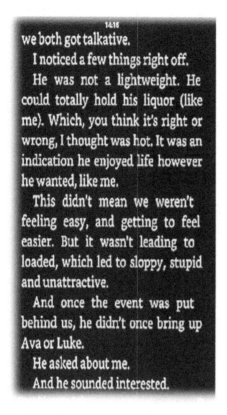
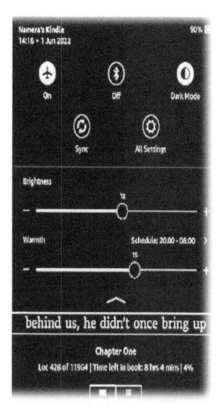

- Swipe down from the upper part of your display to access the all-important settings menu.
- Tap the rightmost icon, which is a half-shaded circle titled Dark mode. And there you have it—dark mode is activated. If you wish to turn it back off, press the button again.

View reading progress

- Tap the Aa button while on a page near the top of the book to access the current progress menu.

- To view your progress in reading, go to More > Reading Progress.

- Hit a method for tracking your progress, then exit the settings by tapping back on the page of your book.

- Checking the time without having to look up from your screen is fantastic, even if you'd rather not see the clock when reading so as not to get distracted.

14:17

we both got talkative.

I noticed a few things right off.

He was not a lightweight. He could totally hold his liquor (like me). Which, you think it's right or wrong, I thought was hot. It was an indication he enjoyed life however

Themes   Font   Layout   **More**

Reading Progress   Time left in book >

Show Clock While Reading   ⬤

Book Mentions
Identifies names of other books mentioned in this book.   ⬤

About This Book
Show information about the book when opened for the first time.   ⬤

14:17

we both got talkative.

I noticed a few things right off.

He was not a lightweight. He could totally hold his liquor (like me). Which, you think it's right or wrong, I thought was hot. It was an indication he enjoyed life however

‹ Reading Progress

○ Page in book   ○ Time left in chapter
   Not Available

⦿ Time left in book   ○ Location in book

○ None

Display reading clock

- To display the time while reading hit the Aa button, then tap More on a page near the top of the screen.

- Then activate the show clock while reading toggling.

- The time will be displayed at the very top of your screen.

- Make sure your Wi-Fi is on, and it will adjust the time for you automatically.

14:17

we both got talkative.

I noticed a few things right off.

He was not a lightweight. He could totally hold his liquor (like me). Which, you think it's right or wrong, I thought was hot. It was an indication he enjoyed life however

| Themes | Font | Layout | **More** |

Reading Progress   Time left in book >

Show Clock While Reading

Set Screensaver as Book Cover

- Enter settings.

- Press All Settings.

- Pick device options.

- Display cover, which will display the book's cover on the lock screen, will be the first option you see on that page.

- To leave the configuration menu, toggle this option on and press the X in the top right corner.

Keep in mind that if your Kindle doesn't display advertisements even when it's locked, this will only work with Amazon books and not with side-loaded ebooks.

CHAPTER 5

Set password

On the other hand, you might be paranoid about anyone else accessing your Kindle at all. A passcode for the gadget is necessary here.

- Enter settings.
- Select Device Options after tapping on All Settings.
- Now you can protect your Kindle with a numeric passcode by selecting Device Passcode.

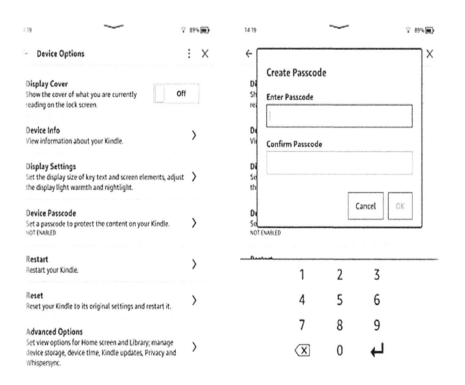

You'll need to input the passcode every time you turn on your Kindle from here on out. If you want to turn it off again, it's as simple as turning it on.

Listen to music

- Enter google play.
- Find the Prime Music app in the menu bar and press it.
- Next to the program, you'll see a green button labeled "Install." Click it. It could take just a few seconds to install.

Excellently! Congratulations, your AMAZON Fire Max 11 now has the Prime Music apps installed. Now you can listen to music right away after opening the app and signing up.

Connect to Bluetooth headphones

- The first step is to go shopping for an AMAZON Fire tablet Bluetooth headphones.
- Use the website HardReset.info to look up instructions on how to pair your specific Bluetooth headphones.

- Use Bluetooth to transmit audio from the AMAZON Fire to your headphones.

Delete cache

- Use the tablet's Power button to switch it off.
- Next, initiate Recovery mode by pressing and holding the Volume Down and Power buttons at the same time.
- Select the option to Wipe the cache partition now. To navigate, use the volume rocker, and to make a selection, press the power button.
- Then, using the same keys, press the Yes option.
- Tap Reboot system now to finish up.

Change Keyboard

Amazon Fire tablets are Android tablets, even if Amazon doesn't want to admit it. That means you have access to the standard Android features, such as customizing the keyboard. We'll demonstrate the process using a Fire tablet.

- First, download a 3rd-party keyboard from the Amazon Appstore or, if you followed our instructions, the Google Play Store.

For this study, we will be using the Gboard keyboard from Google.

- Enter "Settings" once the alternative keyboard has been installed.
- Now navigate to "Device Options."
- You should then press "Device Options."
- Follow this link and click on "Keyboard & Language."
- Go ahead and click "Keyboard & Language."
- To begin using the newly installed keyboard, we must first enable it so that it appears in the available keyboard menu.
- Select the installed keyboard by tapping the "Show/Hide Keyboards" button.
- The keyboard is ready for use at this point. Just click "Current Keyboard."
- From the menu, pick the freshly installed keyboard. Alternately, you can select "Keyboard Settings" to access the preferences menu for the current keyboard app.

- A tiny keyboard icon will now appear in the top bar once you start typing. You can quickly toggle between keyboards by tapping it.

All done! You have effectively shifted to a new keyboard. The default Amazon keyboard is no longer required. Find something more satisfying to do.

Use Gmail

The first approach doesn't call for any app downloads on the Fire tablet. We can take advantage of Amazon's default email client.

- Activate the "Email" app.
- After that, fill in your Gmail address and click "Next."

- Type in your address and click "Next."
- The next page you see is a Google sign-in form. Sign into your Gmail account and click "Allow" to give Amazon access.
- Authorize Amazon to access your account.
- When you're done, you'll see "Setup Complete!" on the subsequent screen. You can now press "Go to Inbox." The synchronization process will take a while.

- You can include a Gmail account in the app by entering menu on the sidebar and pressing "Add Account."
- Select the account type and then tap "Add Account."

Email with Silk Browser

The second option is likewise low-tech and does not need to download any apps. The Gmail website is accessible through your Fire tablet's web browser.

- To access your Gmail account, just use your browser.
- Start by launching "Silk Browser." This is the Amazon Fire tablet's exclusive web browser.
- To access your Gmail account, just visit gmail.com. If you don't want to use the Gmail app, which Google would prefer you to, then press "Use the Web Version."
- All done! The latest version of Gmail's website offers a desktop-like experience.

Uninstall pre-loaded Apps

- This can be done by touching and holding the app on the home screen, and then selecting "Uninstall App."
- To uninstall many apps at once, press "Edit Home Screen" from the menu. Not every software can be deleted.

Remove Home screen Suggestions

You can also want to take away any recommended content from the main menu. These are located in the "Continue" and "Discover" subtabs at the very top of the "Home" tab.

While "Discover" is essentially advertisements for Amazon products and movies, "Continue" is where you'll find apps you've previously utilized.

- When you tap and hold an item in either of these categories, you'll see the options to "Remove from Home" or "Not Interested."

Remove Ads in Lock Screen

- You can accomplish this by visiting the Device Manager section of the Amazon website.
- The "Remove Offers" option will appear depending on the tablet you select.
- If you're looking for a present idea, an ad-free lock screen is available for only $15.

CHAPTER 6

Customize Silk privacy

You should always keep your online privacy and security in mind. Fortunately, Silk provides a number of settings that can be adjusted to suit your needs and keep you protected when online.

- To adjust your browser's settings to your preference, go to the "Privacy and Security" menu.

You can enable or disable secure browsing, do not track, HTTPS, and DNS on Fire TV. If you want to use DNS, you can either stick with your current provider or switch to a more specialized service like Cloudflare, OpenDNS, or even Google. You can also turn on or off Bing suggested searches and individualized suggestions on your Kindle gadget.

Turn on Silk reading view

- When viewing a webpage, check for the "Show in Reading View" link at the page's footer to activate Reading View.
- Simply tapping this region will instantly reformat the website into a more aesthetically pleasing layout.

- This is a great tool for anyone who wants to improve their online reading experience.

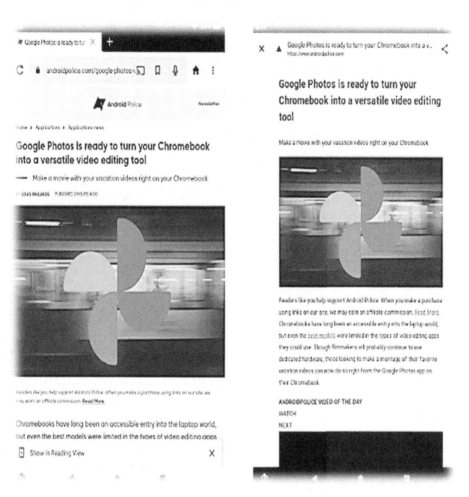

Silk's customize peak row

- Access the browser's settings by clicking the gear icon in the top-right corner.

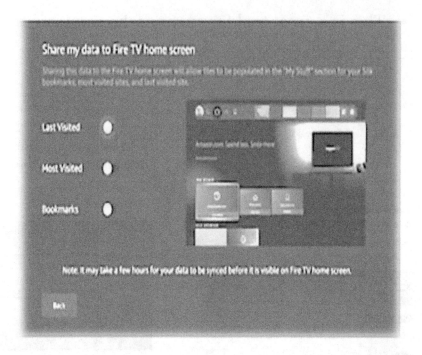

- Choose "Peak Row" and toggle the desired settings on or off. Please be patient as it can take up to several hours for your info to sync and appear on the Fire TV home screen.

- Without even opening up your browser, you can get to your most often visited pages with this handy function.

Switch to private browsing

Your ISP or the websites you visit (including Amazon-affiliated sites) may still be able to see what you're up to.

- Pick the "Enter Private Browsing" button in the Fire TV's address bar to activate the mode.

- Press the 3 dots and click "New Private Tab."

- Returning to the menu bar's 3-dot menu, you can decide to "Exit Private Browsing" on the Fire TV or "View Regular Tabs" on the Max 11 when you're done.

View the desktop version of webpages

- Use the Kindle Fire's menu (three dots) to access the "Desktop Site."

- You can easily return to the standard interface by tapping the icon again and choosing "Request default sites" on Fire TV or "Mobile" on Max 11.

Customize Silk navigation

- In the navigation bar, press cursor navigation and then pick "Spatial Navigation" or "Cursor Navigation".
- Choose "Cursor Speed" from the Silk menu to also modify the pace at which the page scrolls.
- The speed can be customized from the default medium to whatever you choose.

View frequented used sites

- By opening a fresh tab or by pressing the "Home" symbol on the navigation bar, the "Most Visited" part of the Home tab can be enabled on Max 11.
- Then, make sure "Most Visited" is activated by tapping the gear icon in the upper part of the search box. This will arrange your most frequented sites in a row on the Home tab for quick access.

Silk feedback

Feedback from customers is essential to the development of any service or product. The good news is that you can just share your thoughts or report issues on Silk.

- Kindle Fire users can send feedback by pressing the menu button (three dots) and selecting "Send Feedback."
- Enter your feedback, press a category, and decide whether or not to add the current page's URL.
- Your suggestions will be used to make Amazon Silk an even more useful solution for your web surfing requirements.

CHAPTER 7

Set Skype account

- Select "Apps" from the home screen.

- To download the Skype app, go to your device's "Cloud" tab and press the "Skype" option.

- Once you see the green checkmark that means the download is finished, tap the Skype icon to open the program.

- If you already have a Skype account, enter your login credentials; otherwise, press "Create An Account" and fill out the required fields (name, desired username and password, email address, and phone number).

Add Contacts to Skype

- On the main Skype screen, click the button that looks like a person's silhouette with a plus sign, then click "Add Contacts."

- Click the magnifying glass "Search" icon, then choose "Skype Directory."

- If you don't see the Skype name, email address, or full name of the person you want to add, try typing it again and clicking the "Search" option.

53

- To add a contact to your Skype account, tap the contact's name and then tap "Add."

- Type in a personalized message and click "Add."

Make Skype Calls

- From the app's main menu, press "Contacts" to see a list of everyone you've added to your Max 11 HD's address book.

- Select the desired contact, then hit the green "Phone" button to initiate a call.

- A history of recent calls can be viewed by selecting the "Recent" option. To initiate a call, choose the desired contact and then click the green "Phone" symbol.

- Choose between making a call and sending a text message by clicking the "Call Phones" button.

- To make a call, simply enter the number in the top-right field and click the green "Phone" symbol. Instead of calling the number, you can send a text message by clicking the blue "Mobile Phone" button.

Install Libby

Since Libby is not yet available in the Amazon Appstore, Kindle Fire owners can manually install it by using

Overdrive's APK (Android Package File) to sideload it onto their gadget. After that, Once the APK has finished installing, the Libby app will display on your Fire tablet and can be used in the same way as any other app.

- Launch Silk Browser on your Fire tablet and navigate to the Libby APK download page.
- You could see a warning that the Silk browser needs elevated permissions or that you should not open this type of file. Overdrive has verified the download is secure, thus you can ignore these warnings regarding the Libby APK.

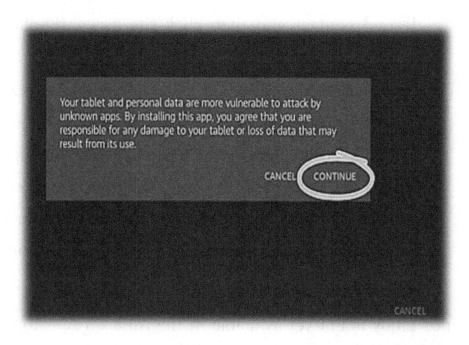

- To continue, press OK, Allow, or Continue. (The phrasing of the cautions may differ.)

- When the download is complete, press Open. (If you're unable to do so at the prompt, navigate to your downloads folder, then tap the file to open it.)

- Go into your device's settings and turn on the option to "Allow from this source" if you are prompted that you cannot install apps from an unknown source.

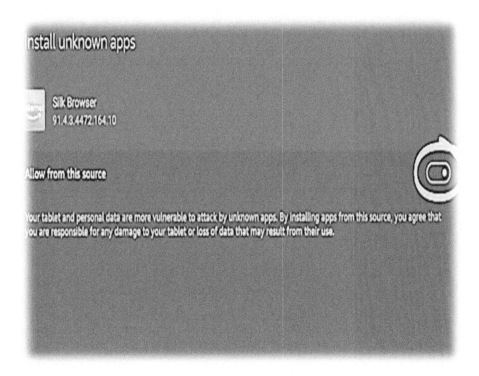

It's important to note that Overdrive suggests disabling this option after downloading the Libby app. You won't

56

have to worry about downloading malicious files unintentionally ever again.

- Click the back button in the upper left corner, then click the Install button.

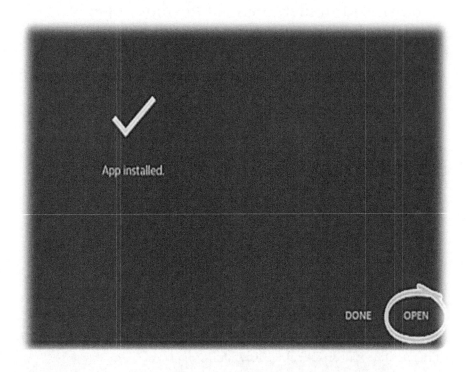

- Press Open once the installation is complete.

Use Netflix App

- Get the app store opened.
- Enter "Netflix" into the search bar, and then hit the Search button.
- Open up Netflix on your gadget.

- To obtain the app for your Fire tablet, press the Download/Install/Get App option.
- Once it is installed, you can launch it by pressing the Open icon.

Configuration

- Launch the Netflix program on your gadget.
- Press Sign On the upper left edge.
- Type in your Netflix account information. Click Sign Up Now to sign up for Netflix if you don't already have one.
- Netflix offers three different subscription tiers. Choose the one that best fits your needs.

Standard: $13.99; Premium: $17.99; Basic: $8.99

- Choose a membership tier and then press the Continue button.
- Choose your preferred method of payment and fill out the required information.
- After subscribing, you can watch Netflix on your Amazon Fire tablet just like any other gadget.

Install YouTube

- You must initially allow tablet installations from unknown sources. To do this, swipe down from the upper part of the screen, then tap "More," and then press "Device."

- Next, activate "Allow app installation." A warning message may appear, explaining that apps not found in the Amazon app store should be avoided at all costs. Activate the 'OK' button;

- Download youtube.apk file from YouTube and save it to your PC.

- Connect your Fire tablet to your computer after the download is complete;

- 'AutoPlay' will now show up on the screen in a few seconds;

- To access files, press "Open device" when the autoplay prompt comes;

- The APK file must be moved to the downloads folder.

- Install ES File Explorer, a program necessary for sideloading programs, then, go to the 'Download' folder. This will provide a list of everything you've saved to your tablet.

- Follow the on-screen prompts to set up YouTube by tapping its icon. Just a moment and the program will be set up for you;

- You can now see if the YouTube app for Kindle Fire has been installed by returning to the home screen. If you have followed these steps correctly, the YouTube app should now be available on your Fire tablet.

YouTube can be accessed quickly and easily on the Fire Tablet by clicking its icon.

CHAPTER 8

Best Fire Tablet Apps

Alarm Clock

When you have an Amazon Fire in your hand, you have no need for a bulky, old-fashioned alarm clock.

- Alarm Clock For Me is a useful program that makes you do everything from setting an alarm to hearing the current temperature and humidity without having to leave the main screen.

- For $0.99, you can upgrade to the ad-free and customizable Pro version, which also removes the app's built-in alarm and sleep music.

Colorfy

- Allows you to press your colors and apply them with a single tap, making it ideal for adults who find coloring books relaxing.
- Some of the more advanced pages need payment, but the basics are always free.

ComiXology

- If you purchased an Amazon tablet for the sole purpose of using it as an e-reader and you enjoy reading comic books, then the ComiXology Comics app(Opens in a new window) is an absolute must-have.

- The software does more than just let you view comics; it also provides a link to a store where you can purchase them.

- We've got you covered if this is your first time reading comics on a tablet.

Disney+

Disney's new streaming service, Disney+, has access to the studio's extensive back catalog. If you have a Fire tablet, you can log in for an account and then use the app to watch every Disney, Pixar, Marvel, Star Wars, National Geographic, and another film ever made. Curious about the initial offerings? If you're looking for anything to stream right now, here it is.

Easy Installer

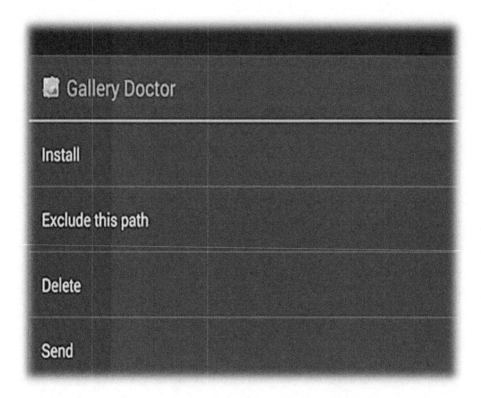

Sideloading APKs is possible with Easy Installer by Infolife (Opens in a new window). This tool facilitates the installation of apps obtained from sources other than the Amazon Appstore.

- To successfully install an application, you will need both the application's APK file and Easy Installer.

- However, software from untrusted sites is more likely to include Trojans and other malware, so proceed with caution.

ES File Explorer

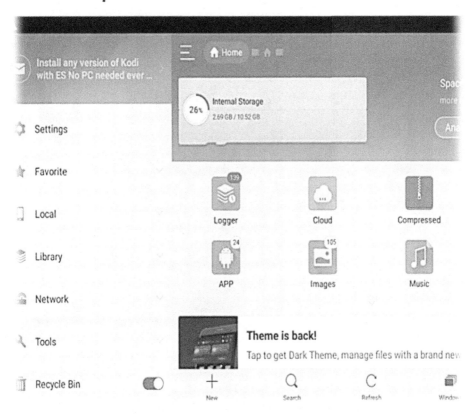

With ES File Explorer, you can easily organize all of the files on your tablet. This cloud-based file organizer provides a centralized location for accessing and organizing your digital files, including programs, documents, and media.

Goodreads

Goodreads is a social app for reviewing, discussing, and rating books; it requires an Amazon account to log in. It's a convenient way to keep tabs on the books you've read, the ones you wish to read, and the ones waiting in your Kindle reading queue.

Homescapes

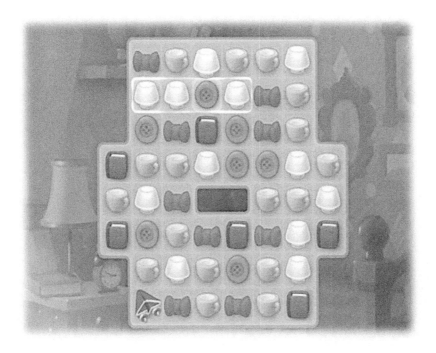

Homescapes is perfect for you if you fancy matching puzzle games but also require a substantial undertaking. You'll need to make pairs of objects to score points and use them to buy new furniture for a crumbling mansion. Gardenscapes will let you restore a garden if you take pleasure in such a focused effort.

iHeartRadio

iHeartRadio lets you listen to your favorite talk radio shows, stand-up comedy performances, podcasts, and sports broadcasts on your Amazon Fire, regardless of whether they are music-based or not.

iHeartRadio

FEATURED ARTIST RADIO

Drake
Siento, The Weeknd, iLoveMem...

Cardi B
Migos, Post Malone, Drake

Post Malone
Juice WRLD, Travis Scott, Rae Sr...

For You

Your Library

Radio

Playlists

Pandora

Pandora, one of the most well-known music streaming services, is compatible with the Max 11 thanks to a free app. You can make custom radio stations including only the songs you've previously decided you like. From there, it will identify music that is close to what you like and play it on repeat for free. Pandora also features comedy-themed channels.

The app is a fantastic resource for discovering new music, despite the occasional interruption from ads (if you aren't on a subscription plan).

AccuWeather

Because it includes so many helpful functions without costing anything, AccuWeather is the finest weather app for Kindle Fire. It's easy on the eyes and keeps information neatly organized. Details such as precipitation levels, cloud cover, sunrise/sunset times, wind speeds, and more are included in the 15-day forecast as well as a minute-by-minute forecast for the next two hours.

Flashlight HD LED

Everyone who owns a Max 11 should download a flashlight app. If you install one now, even if you don't think you'll ever need it, you'll be glad you did. When you initially launch the app or widget, Flashlight HD LED is ready for use. The light can be set to any desired color.

Calculator Plus

One more free app available for the Max 11 is Calculator Plus. It features both standard and sophisticated computation buttons for your convenience. The best feature of Calculator Plus is that it keeps a record of your past calculations, allowing you to review your work without having to jot down the details. The program takes advantage of the Kindle Fire's entire display, making it easier to see and use the controls.

Pinterest

If you're looking for a place to share the things that catch your eye online, go no further than Pinterest, a free social site that makes you do just that. It's fantastic for organizing certain tasks and gatherings. I used it to plan a kitchen remodel by "pinning" pictures of rooms I liked and referring to them later for ideas. Others utilize the site to conceptualize future events, such as weddings, trips, wardrobes, meals, and more through the use of images.

Roku

If you possess a Roku streaming player but hate using the remote, you can get the Fire tablet app instead. In order to cast your favorite material on your TV, you can use the Roku app as a keyboard and digital remote.

Spotify

Listen to any song whenever you like with Spotify. It's free with advertisements, but you can remove them and download episodes for offline listening by upgrading to Premium.

Best Apps for Kids

Khan Academy

The Khan Academy Kids Kindle Fire app is quite well-liked among parents. It's fun to use and instructive for your kid in reading, writing, arithmetic, and reasoning. Books, songs, and games are all available within the app. If you buy a Kindle Fire for Kids, you'll get FreeTime for free. Your child can also access its extensive library of content from other gadgets. Parents can see their children's achievements in the app through a progress report provided by Khan Academy Kids.

BrainPOP Jr

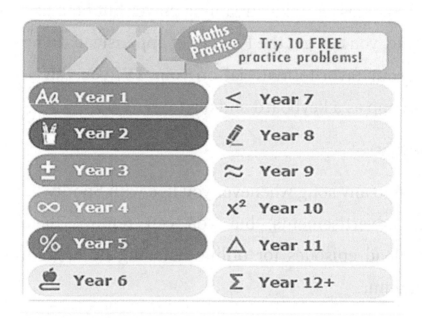

Video of the Week for BrainPOP Jr. Movie of the Week from BrainPOP Jr. for Mobile Devices (Android, iOS).

For kids over the age of three, BrainPop is a must-have Max 11 app. The app's amazing movies and quizzes make learning about a wide range of subjects, like science, math, art, English, and the social sciences, a breeze. A fantastic method for a kid to spend their free time learning something new. It's easy to see why this Kindle Fire app for children would quickly gain popularity, what with its convenient on-the-go movie viewing and quizzes.

Toca Lab

If you own a Max 11, you should check out Toca Lab. Toca Boca, the company behind the software, has won numerous awards for its ability to inspire children's creativity while also providing them with educational benefits.

Toca Lab uses engaging visuals to teach kids about chemistry, making education fun. Instead of learning them at school, your kids can get to know all the elements of the periodic table in a lighthearted way. Virtual testing of these components is also feasible.

ABCya Games

ACBYa is an excellent educational resource for kids in grades K-5. It has a large library of instructional games that are organized by difficulty and age range. This allows students with more advanced skills to choose more challenging tasks. It's also a great spot to hone a talent or discover the best approach to a new skill.

DragonBox Algebra 5+

Dragon Box Algebra 5+ makes it possible for kids as young as five to quickly and simply understand how to solve linear equations. The best part is that kids don't even notice they are learning. Playing Dragon Box Algebra 5+ is easy and entertaining. Children can enjoy this game independently, but adults are welcome to join in the fun as well. It's possible that you'll learn or review some useful arithmetic concepts along the way.

PBS KIDS Games

In PBS Kids Games, your child's favorite PBS KIDS characters star in an educational app available for free on the Max 11. The games incorporate popular children's television programs like Sesame Street, Dinosaur Train, and Daniel Tiger's Neighborhood. Regular updates will bring more games that include kids' favorite characters while teaching them important life lessons in areas like science, math, and creativity.

CHAPTER 9

Alexa compatibility

Send Email Thanks to its helpful features, Amazon's Alexa voice-activated personal assistant has become indispensable to many. If your Fire tablet is compatible with Alexa, your personal assistant can go with you. There are several subtle differences when utilizing Alexa on a tablet as opposed to an Echo gadget.

Read on to find out how to use Alexa on your Fire tablet, both locally and remotely. The Fire tablet's generation determines whether or not Alexa is compatible with it. The generation of the Fire tablet is the same as the manufacturing year.

If a tablet was developed in 2015, for instance, it would be considered fifth-generation technology. Don't get the tablet's generation confused with the number it has as its moniker. The size of the display is indicated by the second digit. Following these procedures will help you determine the manufacturing date of the tablet in question.

- Select "Settings" from the Home screen's app menu.
- Get yourself over to the "Device Options" menu.

- Find it in the section under "Device Model."

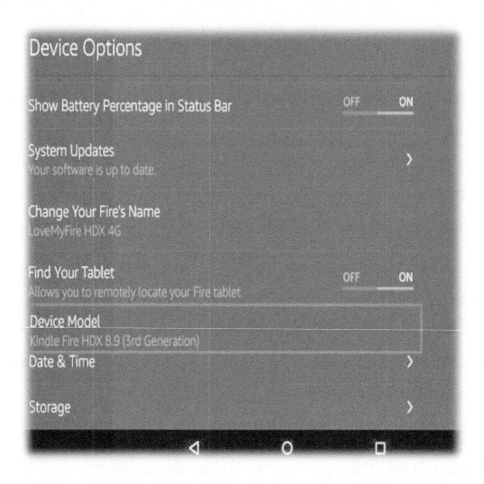

Amazon's voice assistant works with tablets from the fourth generation and later. In addition, Alexa now works hands-free on all Fire tablets released in 2017 and after.

Install Alexa

The Alexa app can be downloaded separately if it isn't already preinstalled on your Fire tablet. How? Read on!

- Access the "Apps" page, and swipe right from the Home screen.

- Search for "Alexa" in the box. You need to get the "Amazon Alexa" app.

These instructions will help you configure the app after it has been automatically installed.

- Hit the "Amazon Alexa" icon from your app drawer.

- To proceed, enter your name and click "Continue."

- If you'd like to use phone verification, you can provide your number.

Communicate with Alexa

- To access the menu, swipe up from the lowest part of the screen, then tap and hold the "Home" button.

- When the blue line begins to light, it's time to ask Alexa.

If pressing and holding the Home button has no effect, it means Alexa is not activated on your Fire tablet. If that's the case, try these solutions:

- Drag your finger down from the tablet's top. Select "Settings" from the menu.

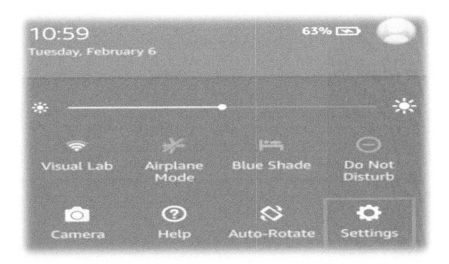

- Click the "Device Options" button.
- To use Alexa, turn on the toggle close to "Alexa."

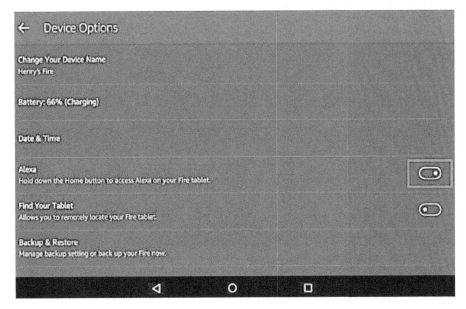

Sometimes the Alexa toggle won't show up in the gadget Settings menu. If it's not on your tablet, the operating system may be out of current and in need of an upgrade. The Fire tablet updating procedure is as follows:

1. Enter "Settings."

2. Press "Device Options."

- Look for the "System Updates" section in the menu.

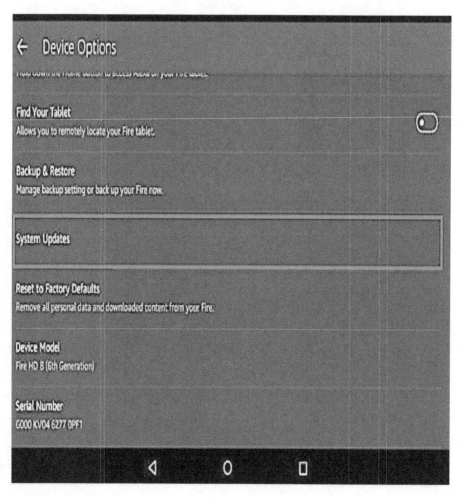

- Press the "Check now" option. To complete the procedure, just stick to the on-screen prompts.

- Once the update has finished downloading, you can activate Alexa by toggling the switch and then calling on her by pressing and holding the Home button. If the line is still absent, turn off any restrictions placed on minors.

Disable Alexa Parental Lock

- Enter "Settings."

- Go to the "Personal" tab and then the "Parental Controls" subheading.

- Type in a password for the Parental Controls and then click "OK."
- Remove the tick from the box labeled "Parental Controls."

Household Profiles
Manage profile settings for child profiles in Household.

Parental Controls
Set a password to restrict purchasing, content types, web browsing, and access to other features. Access to Alexa is blocked when Parental Controls are enabled.

Change Password
Change Parental Controls Password.

Restrict Access for This Profile

Amazon Content and Apps
Blocked: Alexa, Web Browser, Email, Contacts, Calendars, Camera
Unblocked: Amazon Video, Newsstand, Apps & Games, Docs, Amazon Maps, Books, Music, Photos, Audiobooks

Password Protection
Blocked: Playing Amazon videos that you own, Prime videos or Twitch videos; Allowing apps to access your location using location services; Changing Wi-Fi settings
Unblocked: None

Alexa Hands-Free

- When you're at the Home screen, tap the gear symbol to access "Settings."
- Go to your gadget's settings and activate Alexa from there.
- Turn on "Hands-Free Mode" by toggling its switch.
- The wake words "Alexa" or "Amazon" can be used to initiate your digital assistant once hands-free mode has been activated.

Set up Alexa Usage

What Alexa can do for you:

1. Amazon Prime Video.

2. View pictures on Prime Picture.

3. Make use of a timer or alarm

4. Construct a food shopping list

5. Make plans and check the calendar

6. Engage in a video chat

7. Reading on your Kindles.

New uses for Alexa's assistance are waiting to be found. Here's how to get the most out of your Alexa:

- Open up the "Amazon Alexa" app.
- Press "Options" by tapping the three horizontal lines symbol in the upper left.
- The "Things to Try" menu should be chosen. Pick something that interests you and read up on it.
- You can use Alexa for that specific purpose with the help of the app. The following are additional methods for finding Alexa skills:

1. Press the "Skills & Games" tab under "Options."
2. Say "Alexa, suggest new skills."

Use Alexa for reading

Follow these procedures to see if a Kindle book is compatible with the text-to-speech feature:

- Launch the book's product page.
- Check out the "Product details" subsection by scrolling down.
- For the "Text-to-Speech" option, please look there. If the button says "Enabled," you're good to go.

- If you want to utilize Alexa as a reading assistant, try out these commands. You can switch to Audible or another e-book service if you want.
- Just say "Alexa, play the (service) book," then mention the title of the book.

1. Alexa pause my book.
2. "Alexa, stop my (service) book."
3. Alexa, resume my (service) book.
4. "Alexa, read louder."
5. "Alexa, go to the next chapter."

- Tell Alexa end reading in 25 minutes.

CHAPTER 10

Borrow Library books

- You should visit a library that is close to your home. Click the "Library Search" button on the Find Library symbol if you need help locating a library in your area.

- Select the state from the drop-down menu after clicking the map.

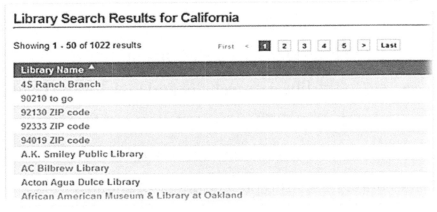

- Pick a library by clicking on it. The Branch Details section of the library's website lists the location.
- You must immediately visit the library and open a new account.

- You will be issued a library card at that point. Creating a password may be necessary. If you need more information, consult the librarian.
- Go to the library's website and look for the OverDrive search portal. This varies between libraries.
- You can also access this URL from the OverDrive library's search page, under "Branch Details."

- Use the search bar to look for books, or press a category to browse.
- Press "Advanced search" and then "Kindle Book" as the format to narrow your results to only Kindle books.
- In order to borrow a book, simply click on it. Borrowing it for your Max 11 is possible if "Available format" lists "Kindle Book."
- When you hit Borrow, a window will appear where the library card number can be inputted.

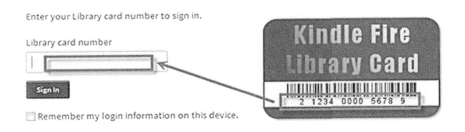

- Then, under "Downloads," pick "Kindle Book."

Bookshelf

Note: Once you select a format, you may only be able to return the title via the software

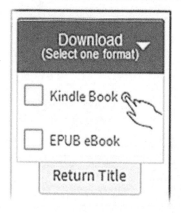

- The link will take you to Amazon, where you might see a similar page. It is the same as buying a book from the Amazon website.
- Pick the Kindle gadget option in the "Deliver to" menu.

- By pressing "Get library book," you can have the book delivered to your Kindle Fire.
- Use Wi-Fi to access the "Books" section of your Max 11. Press "sync" from the drop-down option.

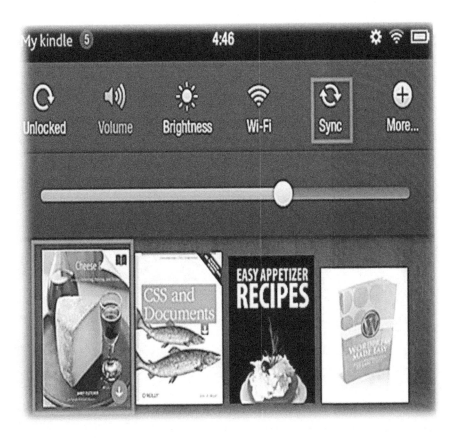

- You can now view the checked-out library book after waiting a few minutes.
- Just one tap and you will have the book downloaded to your Max 11.

Purchase Audible Books via Amazon

The procedures are outlined in detail below.

- First, boot up your Kindle Fire and tap the "Audiobooks" icon on the upper part of the home screen.

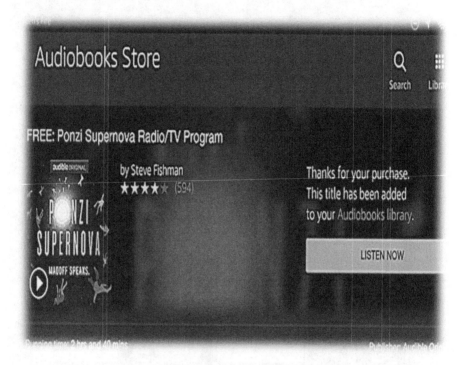

- When you go to your library and press "Audiobooks," you will see all the audiobooks you have bought there.

- New Audible audiobooks can be purchased by clicking the "store" link in the menu bar.

FREE: The Window Man (Unabridged)
By Louise Millar
Narrated by Clare Corbett

- You can either type the title of the book you prefer to buy into the search field, or you can choose one from the "AUDIBLE BEST SELLERS" list. Then buy it by tapping the book's title.

- After a book has been purchased, the user can access it via the cloud by tapping the "library" icon in the app's upper-right corner.

- To download the audiobook, just tap its name.

- Once the audiobook has been downloaded, you can play it even if your device is not connected to a wireless network.

When you return to listening to an audiobook, simply press "Audiobooks" from the main menu and then press the title to begin listening where you left off.

Buy Audiobooks with Audible Account

Your Audible purchases will not appear in your Kindle Fire's Audiobooks library if you have a separate Audible account from your Amazon one. In this situation, you will want to connect your Audible and Amazon accounts.

- First, log in to Audible.com using your existing Audible account information. A prominent "hi, username" greeting will be featured on the homepage.

- From the Hello, username menu, choose "Account Details."

- Second, hit NEW: To integrate your Amazon and Audible accounts, click the button labeled Connect your Amazon account to Audible!.

- After entering your Audible credentials, proceed. Click "next step" after entering your Amazon credentials.

- Finalize your Audible account by entering or selecting a default credit or debit card.

Your Amazon and Audible accounts have been successfully linked up until this point. The Kindle Fire's built-in library of audiobooks will then display all the Audible titles you have purchased. The audiobooks can be listened to by following the steps outlined in Case 1.

Please be aware that once your Audible account has been successfully combined with your Amazon account, your previous Audible login will no longer be valid. So, you will use the same Amazon account information to sign in to your Audible account.

<h3 style="text-align:center">Purchase Books</h3>

- Click the Home button, then find the Kindle symbol. Tapping it will open the Kindle app.

- Pick STORE from the navigation bar at the app's bottom.
- If you want more information about it, you can click here (the link opens in a new tab/window), but if you do not have Kindle Unlimited, you can skip ahead by tapping Continue to store without Kindle Unlimited.

Find a book quickly with the search bar or peruse the many sections. The Kindle app on the Fire HD will allow you to buy any book you find. So long!

First, link your Amazon account with your Kindle.

- Verify the account registration status of your Kindle. To double-check, go to the "Settings" page.

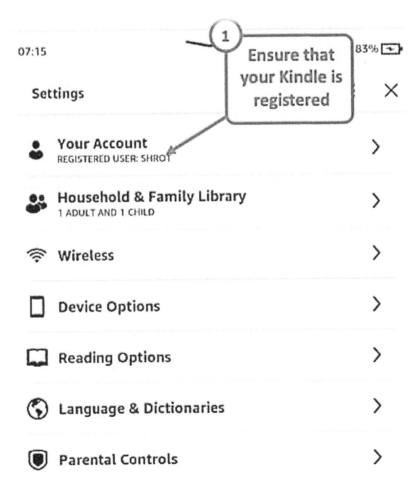

- A registered Kindle will display the account's name in the "Your Account" section. If

Two, set your Kindle to use Whispersync.

- To begin, hit "Settings" from the menu.
- Follow that by pressing "Device Options" from the menu of possible configurations.
- If "Whispersync for Books" is not active, go to "Advanced Options" and turn it on.
- The next thing to do is to access your Amazon account through a computer's web browser.

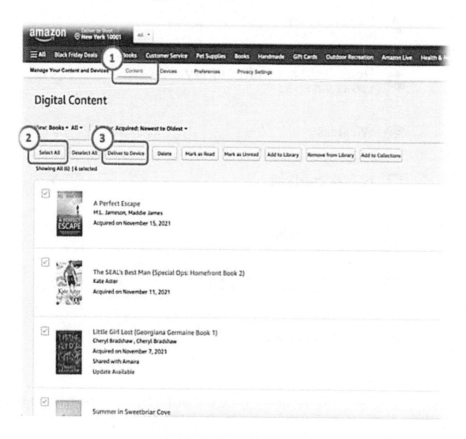

- If you want to access your Amazon "Content Library," click there. After then, a catalog of all the books you have bought through Amazon will appear.
- You may need to click the "content" tab at the top of the page to view the whole list of books. Sign in to the Amazon account you use for reading books.
- Then, choose the Select All icon.

Alternately, you can pick books out one by one. Select the books you wish to move to your new Kindle and then press the "Deliver to Device" option.

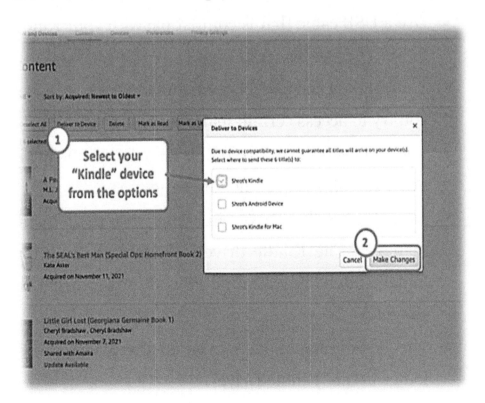

- The final action is to press your Kindle from the list of available gadgets. Because I unregistered my previous Kindle, only the option to press a new Kindle appears here.

- The books will be transferred to your new Kindle within a few minutes after you press "Make Changes."

Move Your Books with a USB cable

- Use the "Download and Transfer via USB" option to save the Kindle books on your PC.

- Use a USB cable that is compatible with your Kindle to link the two devices.

- Your Max 11 can ask for your gadget password when you try to access certain features. Just do it.

- You will need the Android File Transfer utility app in order to link your Kindle Fire to your Mac.

- Launch Kindle Drive in your computer's file manager. The Kindle drive is located in the same folder (often "My Computer") as any other USB gadget.

- The books should be moved to the "Documents" folder in the "Kindle Drive".

- Enter "Internal Storage" on your Max 11. What to do next is to copy all the books into this folder.

- When you are done copying books to your Kindle, press "Eject" from the drop-down menu that appears when you right-click on the drive icon. This allows you to avoid damaging your Kindle's storage drive.

Find your Email Address

The process for locating your Kindle email address on the Max 11 and the Amazon Fire Tab is very similar. However, if you insist on proceeding, here are the directives:

- Enter the "quick settings" menu.

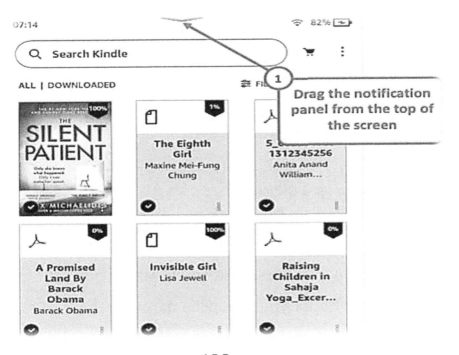

- To access other customization options, press the "More" menu item.
- Then, select "My Account" from the drop-down menu.

- The email address associated with your Max 11 will appear under your gadget's name on the next screen.

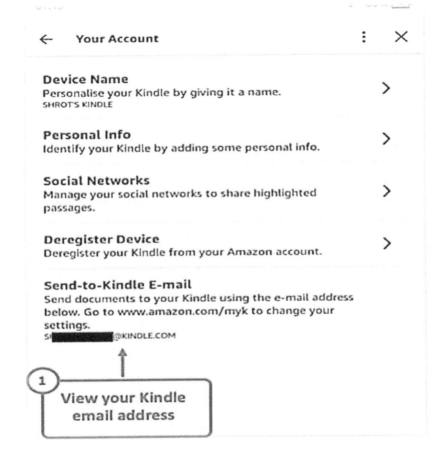

View your Kindle email address

Discover books with the library website

- Visit the library's website and navigate to the OverDrive search page. This may differ between libraries. Alternatively, you can click the link in the Branch Details section of the OverDrive library search.

- Enter a search term into the search box or press a book category. If you just want to search for Kindle books, go to "Advanced search" and choose "Kindle Book" as the format.

- Select the title of the book you want to borrow. If "Kindle Book" is listed under "Available format," you can borrow it on Max 11.
- When you click the "Borrow" button, a box will appear asking you to input your library card number.
- Choose "Kindle Book" from the download menu.
- The website will change to Amazon. It's the same as buying a book from Amazon.
- You can press the Kindle gadget by using the "Deliver to" drop-down option.
- When you press the "Get library book" button, the book will be moved to your Max 11.
- Connect your Max 11 to Wi-Fi and navigate to the "Books" section.
- Select "sync" from the drop-down option. After a few moments, you can view the book you borrowed from the library.
- Tap to download the book, which you can then read on your Max 11.

CHAPTER 11

Take a Screenshot

- Taking screenshots on your Max 11 is simple. Simply press and hold the 'Power' and 'Volume Down' buttons simultaneously for a few seconds.
- The screen will then flicker, and a screenshot notice will appear in the notification area.

Use Quick Settings

- The Fire OS includes a convenient shortcut settings menu. It will be accessible from the status bar.
- Slide down the status bar and then click the 'More' option.
- On the next page, you can discover all of the frequently used 'settings' choices.
- On newer Kindle devices, the 'Settings' icon is located immediately in the status bar.
- By touching on the symbol, you can enter the 'Settings' menu.

Back up data with Amazon Cloud

- On the Max 11, launch the 'Photos' app.

- Then, from the top left edge of the display, touch on the '3 horizontal lines' icon.
- Then press the 'Settings' option.
- You can pick the 'Auto-Save' option there to allow automatic backup.
- You can also pick which photographs and videos to upload manually Manage Notifications on Fire Tablet.

Manage Notification

under Fire OS, notifications are often shown in the notification shade under the fast settings.

- In the settings, you can modify the notification order for each individual app. For example, you must go to 'Settings' > 'Sound & Notification> 'App Notifications'.
- Now, choose the app from which you wish to mute or prioritize alerts. From there, you can choose the appropriate notification settings.

Change Kindle name

- Browse to Manage Your Devices and Content.
- Enters the 'Devices' tab and choose your Max 11 from the list.
- Then, next to the current gadget name, click the 'Edit' button.
- Also, input your desired name and press the 'Save' button.

Uninstall Apps

- Tap Apps from the home screen.

- On the following screen, press the gadget button.

- The apps installed on your Max 11 are displayed. Tap and hold an app icon until the menu appears. Remove from Device should be selected.

- A new screen appears, requesting you to confirm the removal. At the lowest part of the screen, click OK.

- After uninstalling the program, click OK at the bottom of the screen.

- Remove the icon from the home screen if you've added it to your Favorites for some apps.

Find Hidden Camera

Make use of ES File Explorer.

- First, download and install ES File Explorer on the Fire HD. There are other programs for finding files buried behind Amazon's modified Android 4.0, but this one is simple to use and free. You can also get it via the Amazon App Store.

- Install ES File Explorer.

- Launch ES File Explorer and press AppMgr from the top menu.

- Tap Category on the following screen.

- When the Category and Select Types windows appear, press System Apps.

- System Apps will show the apps list. Choose the Camera icon.

- Now, hit the Camera icon and then the Open icon.

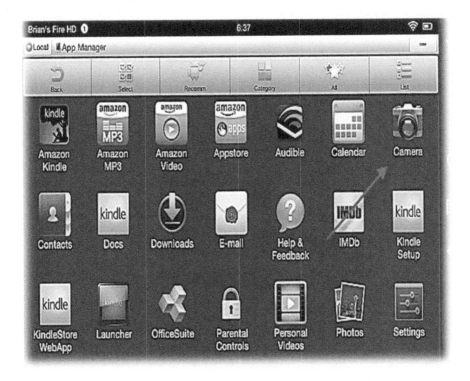

Use Camera

The Camera app appears, and you can begin capturing photos, videos, and panoramic images. It has several effects, a zoom dial, and other choices. Here's an example of video quality settings ranging from 720p to 1080p.

- After you snap your photo or video, you can find it under Photos on your smartphone.
- Alternatively, link the tablet to your PC and navigate to the DCIM folder, then Camera.

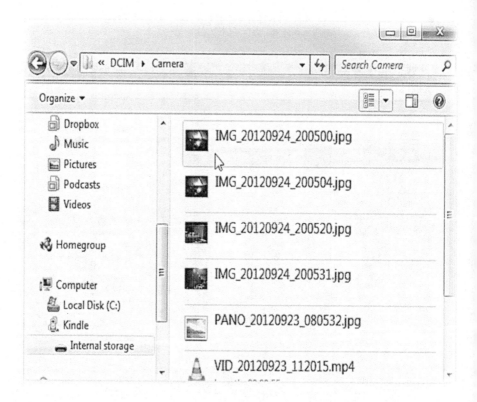

- Taking photos with the front-facing camera isn't practical, and there's no option to create a shortcut to the app. Instead, you'll have to open ES File Explorer every time you want to access it.

Made in the USA
Las Vegas, NV
16 November 2024